TABLE OF CONTENTS

HAPPY HORSES

Horses are farm animals.

They live in the barnyard.

The Barnyard Bunch

HAPPY HORSES

Ryan James

Norwood House Press

Cataloging-in-Publication Data

Names: James, Ryan.
Title: Happy horses / Ryan James.
Description: Buffalo, NY : Norwood House Press, 2026. | Series: The barnyard bunch | Includes glossary and index.
Identifiers: ISBN 9781978574328 (pbk.) | ISBN 9781978574335 (library bound) | ISBN 9781978574342 (ebook)
Subjects: LCSH: Horses--Juvenile literature. | Livestock--Juvenile literature.
Classification: LCC SF302.J359 2026 | DDC 636.1--dc23

Published in 2026 by
Norwood House Press
2544 Clinton Street
Buffalo, NY 14224

Designer: Rhea Magaro
Editor: Kim Thompson

Photo credits: Cover, p. 1 Sabine Hagedorn/Shutterstock.com; p. 5 Denis S/Shutterstock.com; p. 6 Ahaltekin4ik/Shutterstock.com; p. 7 VisualProduction/Shutterstock.com; p. 8 acceptphoto/Shutterstock.com; p. 9 SunnyMoon/Shutterstock.com; p. 10 AllaV/Shutterstock.com; p. 11 Pavel1964/Shutterstock.com; p. 12 Elmari Viljoen/Shutterstock.com; p. 13 Bobs Creek Photography/Shutterstock.com; p. 14 Patrick Jennings/Shutterstock.com; p. 15 SGR/Shutterstock.com; p. 17 Osetrik/Shutterstock.com; p. 18 Michael C. Gray/Shutterstock.com; pp. 19, 21 Rita_Kochmarjova/Shutterstock.com;

Printed in the United States of America

CPSIA compliance information: Batch #CSNHP26: For further information contact Norwood House Press at 1-800-237-9932.

Horse farms have special barns called stables. Stables are divided into stalls. Each horse has a stall.

Farmers take care of stables. They make sure each stall is clean and safe.

HOW HORSES LOOK

Horses are covered in hair. Their hair comes in many colors.

A horse has a **mane** on its head and neck. It has a long tail.

Horses have long legs. Their legs are strong and **muscular**.

A horse has an oval-shaped **hoof** on each foot.

HOW HORSES SOUND

Horses **communicate** with each other. They make a noise that sounds like "neigh."

When horses fight, they make a screaming sound.

WHAT HORSES EAT

Horses are **herbivores**. They eat only plants. Outside, horses **graze** on grass in **pastures**.

Inside, horses eat **hay**.

Horses also eat fruits and vegetables. These foods keep them healthy.

HOW HORSES GROW UP

Baby horses are called foals.

Foals begin to **gallop** just 24 hours after they are born.

FUN ON THE FARM

Horses like to gallop and **prance** around. They also like to play games!

GLOSSARY

communicate (kuh-MYOO-ni-kate): to share information and feelings

gallop (GAL-uhp): to run very fast so that all four feet come off the ground at once

graze (graze): to feed on grass that is growing in a field

hay (hay): long grass that is cut, dried, and used as food for farm animals

herbivores (HUR-buh-vorz): animals that eat only plants

hoof (huf): the hard part that covers a horse's foot

mane (mayn): long, thick hair that grows on a horse's head and neck

muscular (MUHS-kyuh-lur): strong and powerful; having strong muscles

pastures (PAS-churz): grassy fields where animals graze

prance (prans): to use the hind legs to spring forward; to move with high, lively steps

THINKING QUESTIONS

1. What are baby horses called?
2. Where do horses live on a farm?
3. What do horses eat?
4. How do horses communicate?
5. What activities do horses enjoy?

INDEX

ABOUT THE AUTHOR

Ryan James lives in the mountains of North Carolina, where he goes hiking with his dog Bailey. He loves fly fishing, visiting farms in the area, and picking fresh produce. He has always enjoyed writing and wrote his first book as a teenager.